*If you
you're my friend.
Judge Steve Ables*

TEEING UP THE DAY

Stephen Ables

*This book is dedicated to my beautiful and
brilliant wife,
Lynda.
Like Barnabas of the New Testament, God has
given her the gift of encouragement.
Like so many others she has touched,
she always encouraged me
to do more,
to be more,
and to love more.*

Acknowledgements

To my 91-year-old father, who looks more like my brother every day! We never played that well, but our 4-hour talks were the best.

My Pro, Matt Trevino, who has used all the tricks in his arsenal of teaching tools and still can't slow down my swing. Despite that, he's the best.

My kids and their spouses and my grandkids. They are my inspiration for today and tomorrow.

The *Kerrville Daily Times* and their sports editor Jonathan Toye who gave me a corner of the sports page every Friday to share a story.

Riverhill Country Club in Kerrville, Texas. It has been the playground for my family for over 40 years. Like Byron Nelson said, "If I could only play one course, it would be Riverhill."

And the Hill Country Hackers, my soul-mates for over 40 years:

Mike "Mikey" Baumann
Carl "Corky" Browning
David "Burley" Burleson
Phil "Pup" Demasco
Royce "RG" Itschner
David "DJ" Jackson
Dr. Dee "Tex" McCrary
Richard "Racehorse" Mosty
Dr. Chuck "the Glue" O'Donnell
Dr. Rick "Ranger" Schneider
Greg "Cookie" Shrader
Marty "Fast Eddie" Sorell
Stevie "Precious" Ables

Contents

Introduction

I love playing golf for many reasons. The challenge is frustrating but on occasion attainable, which is enough. The setting is beautiful and often breathtaking. But the essence of golf is the camaraderie. Many years ago, I discovered Michael Murphy's book *Golf in the Kingdom*. It is tattered and "dogeared" from constant reference and inspiration and one passage in particular sums it all up.

I quote Agatha the Scottish pub maid, "So Agatha spoke about golf, and the love men have for one another. 'It's the only reason ye play at all,' she said. 'It's a way ye've found to get together and yet maintain a proper distance. I know you men. Yer not like women or Italians huggin' and embracin' each other. Ye need tae feel yer separate love. Just look - ye winna come home on time if yer with the boys. I've learned that over the years. The love you feel for your friends is too strong for that. All those gentlemanly rools, why, they're the proper rools of affection—all the waitin' and oohin' and ahin' o'er yer shots, all the talk of this one's drive and that one's putt and the other one's gorgeous swing—what is it all but love. Men lovin' men, that's what golf is.'"

Michael Murphy says "each of us has a different song to sing in praise of this mysterious game." This is my song.

Teeing Up the Day

A reporter once asked Lee Trevino, "Do you always put your ball on a tee when you are teeing off on a par 3?"

His response, "Why would I ever pass up on the opportunity to start a hole with anything but a perfect lie?"

I agree with Lee, and it made me start to think about my less than perfect way of teeing up my days or rounds of golf. I jump out of bed, quick shower, check the headlines, a quick coffee, and no breakfast, run to the first tee or to my office, take a few deep breaths and watch out world, "game on." However, there were some days that I did a really good job of *Teeing Up the Day*.

For twenty years, I rode a judicial circuit and three weeks of every month, I started my day with a 20 or 30-minute drive. I started turning off the radio and used the drive to give thanks for my beautiful Hill Country, make a few confessions, say a prayer for family and friends, hum a hymn and ask for some wisdom. For me, it was a perfect way to "tee" up my day. I am not riding a circuit anymore, and probably you don't either, but we can still find a way to slow down and make a nice slow swing into this amazing day from a perfect lie.

Cypress

One of the best golfing days of my life was an early fall morning on the Monterrey Peninsula with my dad, my dear friend, and his dad. We were blessed to play Cypress Point. I consider Pebble Beach the High Temple of Golf and Cypress Point as the Holy of Holies. I will never forget walking to the 15th green and my father putting his arm around me and saying, "Thank you, son. I think this is a close as we will get to Heaven on this side of the Bar."

God blessed us with the grandeur of His creation, the gift of a perfect day and the great fortune of sharing the day with our dads. Standing on the 16th tee, I remembered the words of E. E. Cummings:

> "i thank You God for most this amazing
> day: for the leaping greenly spirits of trees
> and a blue true dream of sky; and for everything
> which is natural which is infinite which is yes"

Be Still

*I*t seems the world is too fast. We drive fast, work fast, connect fast, talk fast, eat fast, and leave fast. Mea Culpa. I think it spills over into my golf game. I rush to my ball and hit it as fast as I can before the demons of doubt set in.

A noted golf psychologist told me that he found that great golfers have the ability to slow everything down as they approach a shot and calm their minds of negative thoughts. For about thirty seconds, they would approach the ball with no thought in mind except the shot. He said the most important part of the swing were those few seconds of standing over the shot and being at peace.

The psalmist wasn't a golfer, but his words in Psalm 46 speak to all of us. "Be still and know that thou art God." Be still.

Live Long and Prosper

You can go online and watch a series of short lectures called *Ted Talks*. I ran across one of the talks by a prominent sociologist who talked about the most significant predictors of a person living a long life. The list predictably included good genes, a healthy diet, exercise, moderate alcohol consumption, and no smoking. The surprise factor on the list was the number one predictor. Sitting solidly at number one is "significant social interaction."

If you are looking for an argument for your desire to go play golf and spend some time in the 19th hole having a beverage in moderation, you now have one. So, how about this bumper sticker? "Live long and prosper, play golf with your friends."

Who You're With

The next three weeks hold great promise for me. I am going to visit my son-in-law and then my dad is coming to visit me. In the midst of these visits, I will have the opportunity to sit and walk and talk with each one for four hours because my son-in-law said "Bring your clubs," and my soon to be a 90-year-old dad is bringing his clubs to Kerrville.

When I was younger, the excitement was the game. As I am about to enter my seventh decade, I am excited about a four-hour conversation with people I love.

I read recently a quote from a fisherman. It said, "It is not what you are fishing for, it is who you are fishing with."

I think that says it all.

70 Years Young

About a month ago, my good friend and golfing buddy for over forty years gave me a t-shirt that says, "All men are created equal but the best play golf in their seventies." I love the shirt but what I really like is my friend, Corky, who proved the t-shirt true.

Corky and another longtime friend Tex, are both north of 70, yet they teamed up to win our club's Member/Guest Golf Tournament. At the final hole of the "shoot out" they triumphed over two super young golfers who must still be wondering how they lost.

Judge Oliver Wendell Holmes perfectly described my friends when he said, "To be seventy years young is sometimes far more cheerful and hopeful than to be 40 years old".

Stoops

One of my favorite golfers, Johnny Thornton, tells a wonderful story about one of his octogenarian playing partners. Before a round, his senior buddy loads his pockets with tees. When he hits a tee shot, he always leaves the tee in the ground. Invariably a new golfer to the group will say "Do you want to pick up your tee" and he replies "young man, at my age I've got a lot more tees than I have stoops. I'll just leave that tee for a young man."

Johnny Thornton's friend proves the promise of Job 12:12. "Wisdom is with aged men. With long life is understanding."

I think I will leave my next used tee on the ground. I feel my store of stoops diminishing.

Good Friday

Several Friday's ago, I played one of the worst front nines of my life. I topped drives, hit fat iron shots, and three-putted four times. It was a bad Friday. When I made the turn, I had little hope for a good day. When I started the back nine with a good drive and a solid par, I was a new man and on my way to a miraculous 37. My bad Friday turned into a completely unexpected Good Friday.

About two thousand years ago, one of the worst Fridays imaginable happened in Jerusalem. To a group of loyal followers of Jesus, there seemed little hope that something good would come from the day. Who could have predicted on that bad Friday the world was to change forever.

Thank you, Lord, for taking the worst that could have happened at the hands of sinful men and turning it into the world's greatest victory. Happy Good Friday

Attaboy

I saw my favorite New Year resolution on Facebook. A young lawyer posted that he is resolved in the new year to be "slow to criticize and quick to praise."

I love so many things about golf, but one characteristic that stands out is the first impulse of all golfers to praise and a disinclination to criticize. Not only do we praise good shots, but we find ourselves pulling for our opponents to make the spectacular shot. We might lose the hole, but experiencing a special golf moment seems more important. I think the sincere "good shot" comes from a love for the game.

"Quick praise and slow criticism" in daily life seems to flow naturally from a love for our neighbor. Make today an attaboy day.

Agusta

All golfers dream of making the pilgrimage to Augusta for the *Masters* and all who make the trip will tell you it is a "thin place." It is a place where the distance between heaven and earth collapse, and one senses the majesty and glory and beauty of God's creation spiritually.

When I made my pilgrimage, I was taken by the crowd's reverence. The conversations were civil and hushed and wrapped in smiles. It was a special day, and I remember stopping at a scenic spot and humming the chorus, "Surely the presence of the Lord is in this place."

If you are reading this, my guess is that you are not in Augusta. The good news is that God may give you a "thin place" wherever you may be today, except perhaps a bunker.

Bust a Pipe

In 2016, most of the golfing world suffered mightily with Jordan Spieth as Amen Corner at Augusta, and specifically #12, destroyed his hopes for a back-to-back *Masters Championship*. All of us felt his pain and winced at every missed shot.

My friend Phil has a saying: "Pressure can make water run uphill, but it can also bust a pipe." Jordan surely had his pipe busted that day.

Golf, like all great loves, often produces pressure and suffering, but suffering can either destroy us, or it can give meaning and growth to our lives. I truly believe this, but I sure wish I didn't have so many opportunities for growth.

Small Things

When I go to the practice range, I like to hit full shots; especially my driver. I know the short game is the key to scoring well, but there is nothing very exciting about hitting a 15-foot putt or a 30-foot chip. Harvey Penick points out in his *Little Red Book* this common inclination of all of us to revel in the "big" shot, but he emphatically teaches that the putting green "rats" and chipping green "rats" most often are the most successful golfers.

Jesus' ministry was a ministry of small things. It was a ministry of cups of water and pieces of bread and a gentle touch and a reassuring word. We all know that if we want a successful golf game, we need to start with the small things. Life is kind of the same way. The successful life is a lifetime of looking for small ways to help others.

I read that Mother Teresa was addressing a large group of successful businessmen and made this profound statement: "Very few of us can do great things, but all of us can do small things with great love."

Press On

Shooting a good score in golf requires discipline. Almost every time you play, you will be tempted to hit shots that are inappropriate for your game. How many times have I been in the midst of a good round, hit a bad shot, and then try to make up for the bad shot with a career shot? Invariably the attempt at the career shot gets me in bigger trouble, and I have a terrible hole.

Singer, actor, rapper, and golf lover LL Cool Jay rapped some good advice for the game of golf and life with this wisdom. "When adversity strikes, that's when you have to be the most calm. Take a step back, stay strong, stay grounded, and press on."

Others

Golf fans had a treat watching the final round of this year's *PGA* championship because the leaders all played well. It is wonderful to watch a match where the outcome is determined by good play. As good as the golf was, I was most impressed by what happened when the tournament was over.

Brooks Koepka, after a long walk, was at the door of the scorer's cabin and there was Tiger. He probably had to wait 30 minutes for Koepka, but he was there with a wide smile and a warm handshake and an acknowledgment that it was someone else's day. It is always nice when golf and life teach us that sometimes it is about us, but most the time it is about others.

It made me think of the refrain from an old, old hymn. "Others, Lord, yes others, let this my motto be. Help me to live for others, that I may live like Thee."

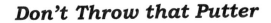

Don't Throw that Putter

Jordan Spieth is struggling a bit this year. Last week he suffered the ignominy of missing a six-inch putt. A friend of mine sent me a list of golf truisms and the first on the list was "Don't ever buy a new putter until you have had a chance to throw it." I am sure that thought crossed Jordan's mind. In fact, he did not throw his putter, and despite a triple bogey ended up two under for the day.

It is not unusual for pros to right their ship during a round, but for amateurs, it is very hard. I find Romans 5:3-4 to be a comforting thought for my golfing struggles. "We also glory in our sufferings because we know that suffering produces perseverance; perseverance character; and character, hope."

Don't throw that putter. Keep hope alive.

The Best Caddy

The best golf is played with a caddy. Recently I was playing a new Tom Doak course that required walking. You can carry your bag, or you can use a pull cart (called a trolley in Scotland) or employ a caddy. I chose a caddy, and he was the best. Jason carried my bag, advised me on distances, read my putts, and always put the right club in my hand.

All those characteristics are common to a good caddy, but Jason went the second mile for me. I was in a bunker attempting a very awkward shot when I lost my balance and wrenched my knee. Jason asked if I needed to quit, and I quickly dispelled that notion. Jason then sat down and took off the brace on his left knee and said, "Put this on. It will give you support to finish the round."

"But what about your knee?" I asked.

Jason replied, "You need it more. Let me put it on tightly," and he carefully placed It on my knee.

As I sat on the edge of the bunker, I had a picture in my mind of the apostle Peter having his feet washed and Christ telling his disciples "I have set you an example that you should do as I have done for you." It was just a simple knee brace, but it was so much more.

Catching Friends

I know I am biased, but I think my golf buddies are some of the most enjoyable guys with whom you will ever play golf. Just last week we were about to start our back nine and came upon a golfer prepared to tee off by himself. He said he was going to play two holes and quit. We insisted he play with us. He ended up playing all 9 holes on the back, and we caught a new friend.

My pastor David in his sermon last week said as Christians, we should always be looking for opportunities to reach out in love to people regardless of their station in life. David said Christ tells us, "If we catch them, I'll clean them."

Fishing on the golf course, I like that.

Almost Perfect

The Wednesday before Thanksgiving is golf day for my family clan. Some of my guys have not hit the ball for months, but their golf hopes spring eternal.

Recently, we almost had the perfect Thanksgiving golf as my oldest son missed a hole in one by two inches. Despite the miss, we danced and shouted and took pictures. If the shot had gone in, we might have referred to that Thanksgiving as the perfect Thanksgiving, but the almost perfect Thanksgiving is probably more appropriate.

Life is better when we realize being perfect is dang near impossible and celebrated near misses are the stuff of a good life and great stories.

The Golf Bug

My son Matthew never caught the golf bug. He loved tennis and soccer, but his golf interest only lasted until we arrived at a stream. Then he went off looking for crawdads, snakes, and turtles.

Matthew has a marvelous ability to resist conforming to the world. There is a wonderful thought penned by Ralph Waldo Emerson that describes Matthew.

"To be yourself in a world that is constantly trying to make you something else is the greatest accomplishment."

That's my boy!

Finishing

President Bush "41" loved to golf and had a passion for playing quickly. He claimed to have the course record at *Arundel Golf Club*. The record was not for the low score but for fast play.

His son said, "Dad loved playing golf, but he was always pushing to finish so he could do what was next."

My father, a very successful businessman, always preached to me that it is easy to start, but finishing is the rub. I am reminded of St. Paul's famous passage in 2 Timothy 4:7: "I fought the good fight, I finished the race, I kept the faith."

I know we can say that about President Bush and my dad. Will someone say that about you and me?

Remembering

One of my dearest friends and oldest golfing buddy lost his beautiful daughter to a condition called aplastic anemia. She was young and beautiful and vibrant and brilliant. She could hit a golf ball a mile and loved to play golf with her daddy. We all loved Amber Dawn, and we do little things to remember her. Her dad always marks his ball with her initials, and we regularly give a drink of water to her tree we planted next to the 18th green.

Golf is all about remembering. I can't remember what I was supposed to get at the store, but I have an elephant like memory when it comes to golf stories. I have found my praying has changed over the years. My young prayers had a lot of asking, but my old man prayers are lots of remembering and heartfelt thanks for the blessings of shared experiences with those I love.

Perform Well

Two recent sand trap experiences reminded me of holocaust survivor Victor Frankl's simple yet powerful truth: "We are in zero percent control of what happens to us, but we are 100 percent in control of our reaction."

Recently a professional golfer, when finally getting out of a bunker, threw a tantrum that a furious five-year-old might have thrown. A week later another professional golfer, had five agonizing bunker shots on one hole. If you were watching, you knew the pro was seething inside and probably wanted to throw a five-year-old tantrum, but he managed to stay composed. I suffered with him and was proud of him at the same time.

In golf and in life, it is wise to remember the advice of stoic philosopher Epictetus: "We are but actors in a play, and it is our duty to perform well the character assigned."

Take Dead Aim

The famous sportswriter Ring Lardner once opined that "if your ball is behind a tree and the tree is skinny, aim right at it. A peculiarity of golf is that what you aim at you generally miss. The success of the shot depending mainly, of course, on your definition of skinny."

As usual, Lardner was looking for a laugh, but if pressed I bet he would agree with Harvey Penick that success begins with a positive target and goal. Before every shot, whether practice or play Mr. Penick preached "Take Dead Aim."

Harvey said taking dead aim is an act of faith. "Your imagination is stronger than your willpower. Your body does what your mind tells it to, and for those few seconds you are what you think."

Confidence

I am excited that we have a lot of young-sters at my course who are taking up the game. Golf, like many things in life, is best played confidently, and confidence gained at a young age is invaluable. I often think of golf psychologist, Dr. Bob Rotella's, assessment that "confident golfers think about what they want to happen on the course. Golfers who lack confidence think about things they don't want to happen."

The eight-year-old who hollered "Judge watch me hit my driver" had no thought of what he didn't want to do. I didn't holler back instruction or a critique. My response was "wow" and "fantastic." I can't teach those kids golf like a pro can, but I can believe and practice what Truman Capote once said: " Anyone who ever gave you confidence, you are in their debt."

Making Memories

When my golf gang is about to play a special course, we say, "Let's make some memories." My latest memories were at *Whistling Straits*; the sight of the 2020 *Ryder Cup*. It was an eighteen hole stroll with caddies, 47-degree weather and winds off Lake Michigan at 20 miles per hour and a new left knee. I shot 92 and loved every step.

That day was another golf memory but every day holds the promise of a special day with your spouse or your kids or a friend or with a stranger. At age 70, I whisper the prayer of Psalm 90:12: "Oh God, teach us to number our days and recognize how few they are; help us spend them as we should."

Witnesses

Last week I almost experienced the worst fear of all golfers. I was playing a twilight nine holes by myself, and on the second hole, I hit a ball straight at the flag. The ball landed a few feet from the pin and to my relief slid just barely by the hole. I almost experienced the worst feeling in golf. A hole in one with no witness in sight.

In many ways, golf mirrors life but not in this instance. The New Testament emphasizes over and over again that our good deeds are not for show and the praise of men but grow out of humility and love for our neighbor. I am all in for humility and love of neighbor, but I think St. Peter will give me a pass for wanting many witnesses and lots of praise for my next ace. Some good deeds deserve to be noticed.

Turn, Turn

One of the hazards of being a devoted golf aficionado is the danger of reading and listening to too many golf tips. I had the opportunity to be in a golf clinic with Earl Woods, Tiger's dad. Most of the clinic had to do with Tiger. Someone asked Earl what instructions he gave Tiger when he was young. The response was immediate, "I reminded him over and over to just open the door and close the door. In other words, just turn away from the ball and turn back to the ball and when he needed to hit the ball a long way just close that door really hard."

Earl's advice to a young Tiger reminds me of Jesus having a clinic with the Pharisees when they asked him what is the greatest of all laws and Jesus answered them in such a simple and profound way. In keeping with the vernacular of Earl Woods, Jesus said, Turn away from yourself and turn to God and your neighbor." Turn, Turn. So simple yet so profound.

Golf Stories

I have been asked several times if I am running out of golf stories. I am not positive about this, but golf stories may be infinite. Just last week, I was having a conversation with my friend and colleague Mickey, and he shared with me that he was celebrating his 48th anniversary. I looked at him quizzically and told him there was no way he and Karen have been married 48 years. His answer gave birth to another golf story.

"It's not my wedding anniversary, he said. This is the 48th anniversary of my first hole in one."

He then told me where and how it happened. Truly a man after my own heart. He did tell me he never forgets his wedding anniversary and of course, his wife and daughter are more important than golf, but he does have a trophy commemorating his hole in one and he is hoping his wife will let him display it in a prominent place in his new house. I wonder why they call us golf nuts?

A Good Hug

It is hard to know what to say to a golfer who is having a terrible round or just finished a horrible round. It is particularly difficult for family members to console the disappointed golfer who is contemplating throwing his clubs into a trash dumpster.

My wife and I have a process for handling my bad rounds. When I come in the house she says "How did you play?" and if I say "it's a beautiful day," there is no more talk of golf. Nongolfers don't understand that when we play badly, we are sure God is punishing us for something we have done or said.

For all you folks who have encountered the disconsolate golfer, the best response is found in Proverbs 12:23: "Anxious hearts are very heavy, but a word of encouragement does wonders." Sometimes we just need a good hug.

What a Great Game

The game of golf is a game of personal integrity and civility. It is dependent on the trust of your opponent and flourishes when you are respectful and supportive of your adversary. The match begins with a handshake and a sincere wish of good luck and proceeds with a conscious commitment to civility. The round ends with a respectful removal of your hat and a firm handshake with your opponent and a meaningful thank you for the experience.

If you have a copy of the USGA rules of golf, the first section is titled etiquette and states, "The overriding principle of golf is that consideration should be shown to others on the course at all times." What a great game.

Don't you wish we could play politics like we play golf?

Calming the Storm

There are many things in life that are totally exasperating, and golf is definitely one of them. The game can drive you to the brink of insanity.

As a young man, I tossed a few clubs, and as an old man, I still voice a few inappropriate words. The truth is we all lose our cool, and even the most devout Christian will have moments of visible consternation. I think all of us would like to find some calm in the midst of our occasional storms.

Theologian Leonard Sweet said when Jesus and his disciples were in a small boat being cast about on the sea, the miracle was not so much Jesus calming the storm but the miracle of calming those in the storm. I need to remember that the next time I top my drive into the creek.

Bringing Out the Best

When I play golf with my pro, I nearly always play well. I am inspired by his good play and calm demeanor. It is like when my kids were growing up, I always encouraged them to look for friends who would make them better people and not drag them down. We call people who lift us up and make us better, "balcony people."

I think one of the best compliments a golfer can receive is another golfer saying, "I always play better when I play with you." I can't remember where I heard this, but I believe it. "My best friend is the one who brings out the best in me."

Partners

When I play in a partnership golf tournament, the following is a close approximation of the discourse in my brain. "Dear God, don't let me let my partner down. God, please don't let me start shanking the ball or get the yips on all my three footers."

In anticipation of this standard partner angst, I have looked for and found a Bible verse for all golf partners as they approach their match. It is from the Old Testament wisdom literature found in Ecclesiastes 4: 9-10: "Two are better than one because they have a good return for their work. If one falls down, his friend can help him up. But pity the man who falls and has no one to help him up."

Amen and amen.

Confidence

My 90-year-old father is coming to town next weekend to be my partner in the club's annual partnership putting contest. Dad never knows how hard to hit the ball on our extremely fast greens. He will always take a practice stroke and says, "Stevie, is that stroke about right."

Truth be known, I am never sure if I am telling him correctly, but I always confidently assure him his stroke is beautiful. I may not give him the correct measure of the stroke, but my answer exudes confidence. I always say, "Dad, that stroke is perfect, knock it in the back of the hole."

I am with the famous golf instructor Bob Toski who says, "Most golfers prepare for disaster. A good golfer prepares for success."

And so does a good son.

Grounding Arnie Putter

My golf buddy Frank died an untimely death at age 56. Frank loved golf, and much of his golf gear was at his funeral. At the front of the church right in front of the pulpit was his putter, which he named "Arnie Putter."

Frank had a love/hate relationship with Arnie and frequently would heave his putter in disgust. Actually, he threw Arnie so much that Frank's friends applied for and got a Delta frequent flyer card for Arnie. If you go to Fair Oaks Country Club you can see Arnie and the frequent flyer card hanging on the wall.

Frank went to a spiritual retreat not long before his death and during a service called dying moments, he told me he wanted to give up the anger he had in his life, and he would start with not throwing Arnie any more. I don't think he threw Arnie again.

I think Frank would have liked it if when we think of changing bad habits in our lives that we are inspired by his grounding of Arnie Putter.

Gossip the Gospel

No one likes to tell a story like a golfer. The group of golfers I play with gather once a year to celebrate the prior year. The presentation of the "Shot of the Year" is one of the high points of the evening. We can't wait to share new stories, describe new courses, and relive old tales.

I'm an unrepentant "golf gossiper." I can't wait to tell someone my latest story and listen to the stories of others.

Theologian Dr. Leonard Sweet feels the fate of the church rests with the church's decision as to whether it will get excited about the gospel story and find every occasion to "gossip the gospel." The prospects for the church are exciting if we "gossip the gospel" as well as we gossip our golf.

Be Still

Type A personalities, like myself, tend to have a tumultuous relationship with golf. The only time I have a deliberate, rhythmic tempo is when I am ill and on prescribed medication. Several days ago, I was working on my terribly inconsistent putting. After about 10 short misses in a row, I stopped and tried to figure out what I was doing.

I decided to concentrate on keeping my head still. It really helped to slow down and be still. It is contrary to my nature to be still about anything, but sometimes we need to be very still for God to speak to us. I am thinking of using Psalm 46:10 as my new swing thought. "Be still and know that I am God."

Golf is Hard

If you don't already know this, I will let you in on a secret. Golf is hard. It is frustrating and fickle and fraught with abuse. Despite this, our passion for the game is brilliantly displayed in the commercial where four guys are driving home from golf, and one golfer is furious with his game all the way to his driveway. When he is dropped off, he calmly looks to his golfing friends and cheerfully says, "Same time next week."

My preacher nailed it last Sunday. All the things we really love require effort. Marriage, parenting, occupations, and yes, golf. When you love something, you commit to the struggle because you know the rewards will come.

High Praise

Back in the early 80s, Byron Nelson spent many weekends in Kerrville at *Riverhill*. Mr. Nelson designed the *Riverhill* golf course with his good friend Joe Finger. Sometimes he would play on Saturday morning, and our young golf group on occasion got to play with him.

One Saturday morning, my good friend Richard teed off on the 3rd hole with a one iron. It was a spectacular shot, and Byron Nelson said: "Son, that's as good a one iron as I've ever seen on the tour."

It was a "Wow" moment. Someday when Richard's eulogy is read, I anticipate the "One Iron" story will be told. What a gift, the gift of high praise. Taking the time to recognize and compliment and praise another may seem insignificant, but to the recipient, it may the most treasured gift of their life.

Carpe Diem

I played golf last week with my new friend Greg. Greg had a serious stroke about a year ago. He had brain surgery and has been on a slow, tedious rehab. We played 9 holes, and he duffed most of his shots. Despite his poor balance and duffed shots, he was smiling and laughing for two hours. I had the feeling he was just glad to be there.

On the 8th hole, he rammed in a 15-foot putt to save bogey, and we fist bumped and high fived like he won the Masters. I have seen a lot of good shots, but that one goes on my "favorites" list. When we walked off the green on nine, he looked at me and held up his thumb and said, "Carpe Diem." Way to seize the day Greg. Thumbs up back at you.

Making Friends

There are many ways to make friends. We make friends at work, and school, and church, but for my money, golfers enter into friendships quicker than most. I think the key ingredient is that a golfer is immediately in a situation where there are shared successes and failures. We are attuned to our own game, but a large part of our round is focused on our playing partners.

I don't think the famous English lawyer, judge and author Thomas Hughes was a golfer, but he could have been talking about us and the game when he said, "Blessed are they that have the gift of making friends for it is one of God's best gifts. It involves many things, but above all, the power of going out of one's self, and appreciating whatever is noble and loving in another."

Small Things

With the onset of morning freezes, the golf fairways and Bermuda greens are going dormant. To most golfers, this is disappointing as they miss the green replaced by brown and the fairways have become thin and hard. For me and my friend Phil, it is a much anticipated time of the year as our normal drives of 180 yards are now rolling out 20 to 30 yards longer. We are big hitters again!

Truth be known, these "big" drives will not help us that much. If we score well, it will not be because of an occasional long drive, but because of our attention to small things, like chipping, and putting, and recognizing our limitations, and making wise decisions.

Our salvation depends on us doing the small things well. Sounds a lot like life, doesn't it?

Being Responsible

Being a quintessential fair-haired, red-faced Irishman, I go for regular checkups with my dermatologist. My last exam produced four big scabs on my face where doctor burned off four pre-cancers.

My dermatologist wants my golfing attire to be long pants, a long sleeve shirt with the collar turned up, a very, very wide-brimmed hat, and the highest level of sunscreen on the market. He also wants me to wear gloves on both hands and to start playing at daybreak and quit before nine a.m. I told him I would consider his request, but don't count on it.

The bad news is that I know he is right. Things we enjoy including golf can have downsides. It can keep you away from your family. It can interfere with your work, and if you play in the middle of the day during the heat of the summer without sunscreen, it may kill you!

God, help me today to be responsible about the things I love, including golf

Thanks Mom

My mom gets a lot of credit or blame for my love of golf. When I was 11, Mom took me to the old red brick Sears store in Dallas to buy my first real set of golf clubs. I touched every club in the sports department before settling on the *Doug Ford Signature* set of clubs. They included a 3, 5, 7, 9, wedge, 3 wood, and driver. I picked out a putter that looked like Arnie's. She also bought me the ugliest pair, solid black golf shoes out of the bargain bin.

We didn't have much money, but my mom decided to give wings to my golf dreams. Mom has passed, and I don't think I thanked her enough for that day. On Mother's Day weekend, I remember the counsel of the Book of Proverbs, "Let your parent's wisdom guide you wherever you go and keep you from bringing harm to yourself. Their instruction will whisper to you at every sunrise and direct you through a brand new day."

Thank you, God, for loving Moms and Dads who give wings to their children's dreams.

Don't Be a Flogger

Golf spelled backward is flog which is unfortunately very appropriate as most golfers feel compelled to flog themselves on a regular basis. I think it is admirable to have high expectations but face it, golf is a difficult game.

Recently an "out of towner" played with our group and shot a respectable 80. I would have been bragging, but this six handicap was mortified that he had played so poorly. He was a true "flogger."

God, give me high hopes, realistic expectations, and a pleasant disposition about golf and especially life.

Plugged In

Years ago when I bought my first golf cart, I made a big mistake. My batteries started going down and I replaced them one at a time. Unbeknownst to me, the new batteries surrounded by the old batteries began to overcharge trying to compensate for the lack of power from the old batteries. The new batteries wore out in an abbreviated time because they had no support. It was connected to a defective power source that quickly drained it of its power.

How many defective power sources are in our lives. Probably too many. Thank you, God, for the positive power of Your Grace. Thank you for the power of loving families and faithful friends. Keep us plugged into you.

Parables

This is club championship week. Everyone has a steely look of resolve in their eyes. Tonight there will be a dozen club champion "wannabes" on the practice range pounding out balls. Everyone will be looking for that extra muscle memory to compensate for involuntary emotional twitches.

I plan to hit a few balls myself, but I have a new strategy this year. I am going to keep a notepad and record all the notable events of the weekend. Bad breaks, yanked putts, Duck hooks, and the occasional good shot will be jotted down. I anticipate my playing partners will look at me quizzically when I occasionally say, "What a great opportunity for a story!" Instead of Arggggh.

The glory of the good shot is passing, but the treasure of a good golfing parable is a prize that lasts a lifetime.

In Between Time

One of my best rounds of golf took place in New Mexico. My buddy Chuck and I arrived the day before the rest of our playing partners, and we decided to get in a round at *The Links of Sierra Blanca*. As we teed off, the dark clouds broke, and the most beautiful mountain day emerged.

Doc and I seemed to have the course to ourselves. We walked and told stories, laughed, sang show tunes, looked at flowers, watched birds, hit long drives, made good shots, and laughed off the bad ones.

It reminded me of Michael Murphy's *Golf in the Kingdom*. I have page 178 "dog eared" where Sivas Irons in response to Michael's failure to recognize the walking part of the game says, "well, it's too bad....'Tis a rotten shame, for if you can enjoy walkin', ye can probably enjoy the other times in your life when you're in between. And that's most the time, wouldn't you say?"

Doc and I experienced "in between time." It was a special day, and I don't have a clue what I shot!

Say a Prayer for My Driver

In golf, like life, there are certain things we are good at and other things where we struggle. Some analysts felt the wedge around the green was the weakest part of Jack Nicklaus' game, but a golf analyst pointed out it was hard to tell because he never missed a green.

I am currently in a prolonged driver slump. First, I am like Arnold Palmer, who said several years ago, "I am hitting my driver so short, I can hear the thump when it lands." Second, every ball in flight is different. The good news is I know my weakness, and I am seeking help.

In golf and life, recognizing our weaknesses is the first step to recovery. I like to start with prayer, and I am saying a prayer for the weaknesses in my life and my driver. Feel free to say a prayer for me (and my driver).

Buried in Our Head and Heart

Well-known Hill Country golf enthusiast Bob Matjeka passed recently. He was a "Golf Pharisee." The term Pharisee is derogatory to some, but in my context, it is a compliment. Bob loved the game of golf and had a strong attachment to the rules of the game. We all tried to stump him with obscure rule questions, but we were seldom, if ever, successful.

One of Bob's golf buddies suggested that a copy of the *Rules of Golf* needed to be buried with him, but another observed they were already being buried with him deep in his head and heart. Despite his great affection for rules, I know Bob would have agreed that loving people is more important than keeping rules—but, hey, who says we can't do both.

Saving the Lost

Have you ever come across a mother lode of golf balls? My most memorable experience of golf ball finding happened at *The Quarry Golf Course* in San Antonio. On the 17th hole, you play along the ledge of an old granite quarry. If you hit the ball left, your ball is lost over the edge of a 100-foot sheer cliff. Of course, I hit my ball left.

When I peered over the edge, I saw balls everywhere. The problem was there was no easy way to get to them. On this day we had no one behind us, so I headed down the hill. I found at least two dozen almost new golf balls. It was a strange experience—a field of lost golf balls, plainly visible, and ready to be rescued by someone willing to take the time and experience some discomfort to save them.

I think Jesus could have made a parable out of this.

Let's Celebrate

Recollections of great moments in golf are often punctuated by a vivid moment of celebration. I remember Jerry Pate's plunge into the water off the 18th green at *Sawgrass* after winning the PGA, Jack Nicklaus doing a poor imitation of Michael Jordan with his three-inch leap to celebrate his birdie on the 16th hole at *Augusta*, and Tiger's uppercut fist pump on the same hole after a spectacular chip in.

One of my favorite memories is Hale Irwin giving high fives to the entire gallery at the *Olympic Club*, and I will never forget the image of Bill Murray dancing with an elderly lady in a bunker at *Pebble* after holing a sand shot. I love celebrations, and it drives me crazy when a golfer does something incredible and acts like it is commonplace.

As we head into the new year, I am hoping for some great moments of celebration in golf and in life. I resolve to celebrate and cherish those who bring joy to my life.

It's the Game

One of my old friends, C.J., achieved a lifelong ambition of going to Scotland to play golf. He played *St. Andrews* and a few others and was nearing the end of his trip. He stumbled upon a small course that had a tiny clubhouse. When he walked up to the clubhouse, four old Scottish gentlemen were sitting out on benches passing the day. C.J. asked if he could play a round on the course.

The old men could tell he was an American and sized him up as a tourist and told him the course was not much of a course and he probably wouldn't enjoy it. C.J., in a moment of inspiration told them, "Ah, but it is not so much the course, it's the game." The old Scotsmen took to him immediately. They told him to stay out on the course and have a pint with them when he finished.

It was a great day! I think C.J. would agree with me that golf is just like life in that success is often getting what you want, but happiness is wanting what you get.

An Extra Long Retriever

My wife gave me an extra long ball retriever. It will almost reach farther than I can see in the water. I drive my playing partners crazy as I beeline for every water hazard and slowly drive the shoreline before approaching the hole.

The more I look for lost golf balls, the better I get at it. I find them in very unlikely places, and I will notice them when they have been overlooked by everyone else. It takes some experience to begin to notice those small white objects almost lost to the world.

There are a lot of people like golf balls in a hazard. They are on the verge of being lost forever but for the possibility that a fellow human being is experienced is looking for them and has a desire to rescue them. Most often, the problem is they are so far away; it takes more than a human reach to bring them up.

I think God wants us to be on the lookout for people in need. Perhaps in some small way, we can be their extra long retriever to bring them back to the surface of life.

Growing Up

Recently I had some really bad luck on the 18th hole. I was playing a decent round, and on the last hole, I hit a fair drive, almost to the corner of the dogleg. My second shot almost missed the tree at the corner but alas, it didn't, and my ball took an incredible 30-yard cargo left out of bounds.

After a half-century of golf, I may be growing up. Miraculously, I did not get mad. As a matter of fact, I made a joke. I told my playing partner, "if I had bounced in the trap, I would probably make a triple bogey." I then dropped my ball and hit a nice draw to the middle of the green and snaked in a 25 footer for a bogey. I walked to the 19th hole like I had made a birdie.

Thank you, God, for giving me a teaching lesson on maturity, even if it were 50 years later than it should have been.

Encouragers

It has been said many times if you want to observe the true character of a person, play a round of golf with them. After four hours of hitting, riding, talking, and scoring, you begin to see a person's true colors.

Not long ago, I observed overt rudeness by a player toward other players and particularly toward an assistant pro. I asked the pro about the man and his rudeness, and she gave a most descriptive response in her proper English accent, "The gentleman has some endearing qualities, but he does not show them very often!"

This golfer should have followed the advice of Goethe, who said, "It is ever true that he who does nothing for others does nothing for himself."

I like the endearing quality of a person who believes a word of encouragement does wonders for the encouraged and the encourager.

Precious Memories

L ike most golf nuts, I have a collection of logo golf balls, from the many courses I have played. Often I will look through the collection, and my mind takes me back to the majesty of *Pebble Beach*, the elegance of *Pinehearst*, the unmatched beauty of *Cypress Point*, and this week, the mystique experience of walking *August* (not getting to play the course but following the pros as they played the Masters).

I can spend an entire evening remembering golf outings with my buds and hours of talk that generally begin with, "Do you remember."

The grand thing about golf is that you may play a course only once, but you can remember it forever. We are approaching Maundy Thursday and Easter. Jesus ate with His disciples, and He told them, "When you eat this meal, remember Me."

No telling how many times Peter and John started an evening with "Do you remember." I don't thank God enough for the precious gift of remembrances. I may hum an old Gospel hymn today: "Precious memories, how they linger; How they ever flood my soul. In the stillness of the midnight; Precious sacred scenes unfold."

A Good Bounce

My buddy Burley gets more good bounces than anyone I have ever played with. I have seen him get more good bounces in one round than I get in a month. My golf group often calls an opportune break, "a Burley Bounce."

One time I asked Burley about his uncanny good luck. He explained that he hits the ball very straight because even his bad shots are headed at the target. There's a chance for good to happen. Burley summed it up by saying, "Steve, it's hard to get a good break when you are not moving toward the target."

I would like to live like that.

You can't expect good things to happen in golf or life if you are aimed in the wrong direction.

Get Off the Merry-Go-Round

My daughter was always nervous about starting a new school year. She couldn't figure out why she was so nervous about something she really loved and was looking forward to starting.

Every golfer in the world knows exactly how she felt. The combination of exhilaration and dread that follows a golfer to the first tee of a tournament is palpable. How can something you love and look forward to doing cause so much anxiety? It seems that's the way God created us. Everything worth loving can and probably will subject us to "roller coaster living." Ups and downs, excitement and discomfort, anticipation and dread, but seldom, if ever, dullness.

Personally, I'm opting for pursuing the loves of my life. I'd rather ride a roller coaster any day rather than a perpetual merry-go-round.

Balcony People

L ast week I had the pleasure of playing a quick nine holes with my wonderful club pro, Matt. He is an outstanding player and teacher. Generally, when we play, he sees a multitude of issues in my swing, but not this time. I only miss-hit a couple of shots and scored well.

I told Matt that through the years, I tend to play better when I play with good players. Their play tends to inspire me. Isn't it true in life that when we surround ourselves with sweet, loving people, we are better? I call these friends "balcony people" because they lift me up. I hope you have lots of balcony friends in your life. If you happen to be one of my balcony friends, thanks.

A Good Bounce

Two weeks ago, I made my third hole-in-one on the 11th hole of my club. This hole in one was from the senior gold tees. Thirty years ago, I made a hole-in-one on the same hole from the championship tees. Fifteen years ago, I aced the 11th from the white tees. If I live for 15 more years, I think the ladies tees will be my ticket!

I feel fortunate to tell this story because I have dear friends who are ten times better than me who have never made a hole-in-one. Golf and life are so often very unfair. This old-timer who is destined for the ladies tees, got a really good bounce two weeks ago.

My hope and prayer this week is that a really good bounce will be all yours.

A Golf Course and a Convertible

One of the great positive thinkers of literature is the classic cartoon character, Charlie Brown. Charlie was visiting his good friend Linus and tells Linus that when he grows up, he wants to own a convertible and a golf course and thereby always be happy. When Linus asks how come, Charlie Brown replies, "That's simple. If the sun is shining, I can ride in my convertible with the top down, and if it's raining, my golf course is getting watered. Therefore, I'll always be happy."

Life is a bit more complicated than Charlie's formula, but it is amazing how much a positive, confident perception of your golf game and your life gives you a good start on success and happiness. Worry will destroy many a golf swing and lots of our days.

Like my dad always says, "The only thing worry waters is a disaster."

Play All Day for a Dollar

I taught myself to play golf on a municipal golf course a few miles from my aunt's house in Seagoville, Texas. Aunt Barbara would make peanut butter and jelly sandwiches for my buddy Barry and me and take us to the golf course early in the morning. We would play all day for a dollar.

There was a big pecan tree next to the putting green where we would eat our sandwich and drink an *R.C. Cola* on our brief lunch break. We tried to hit every shot just like Arnie and often pretended we were playing on *Shell's Wonderful World of Golf* at some exotic place like the *Zimbabwe Country Club*. It is hard to imagine North Central Texas as the *Zimbabwe C.C.* Unless you are 12 years old with a brand new *Doug Ford Signature* driver in your hands.

Thank you, God, for the limitless joys of our youth and thank you for golf buddies who help us find moments to recapture it.

Take Your Best Shot

It is fun to play "best" game. You know, what's the best movie you ever saw, what's the best meal, what's the best golf course? One of my buddies asked me, "What's the best golf shot that you ever made."

It May have been a pressure putt. I was playing the final round of the second flight of the club championship. I was down by one on the last hole, and I had a 30-foot putt for birdie to extend the match. I knocked it dead into the hole.

The rest of the story is my opponent then knocked in a 25-footer for birdie to beat me. I took my best shot and lost. Sometimes our best shot is not enough. That's golf and life. My prayer is that I will take my best shot at life today, but if I come up short, I will feel God's Grace and assurance that I am loved.

Raise Up a Child

For my money, the best rounds of golf are with your parent or child. I am so fortunate that my 91-year-old dad and my 46-year-old oldest child are often golfing partners.

I played with a father-son duo this past weekend. Rick and his son Matt were my partners. Early in the round the Dad uncharacteristically missed two short putts for birdie. When his son missed one later, we consoled him with the assurance that it was not his fault. It was obvious he inherited his dad's putting stroke. We were joking but watching Rick and his son, I was reminded of Proverbs 22:6: "Train up a child in the way he should go and when he is old he will not depart from it."

Play a round with Matt, and you will know his dad raised him right. Sometimes Proverbs 22:6 doesn't work for putting, but it is surely true about life.

F Before G

I saw a bumper sticker that read, " My wife said if I go golfing one more time she'll leave me. God, I am going to miss her."

Wives get a bum rap over golf. Most golfing jokes are at the expense of the poor wife's inability to remain calm and cope with her husband's crazy golf passion. I have the most understanding wife in the world. Catch this. For one of my birthdays, she saved money for a year to surprise me with a golf trip to the Monterey Peninsula. Eat your heart out, fellow golfers.

However, even though she is the most understanding and caring wife on the planet, I still drive her to the brink of insanity with my occasional lapses into gross self-indulgence over golf. All of us crazy golfers need frequent perspective checks. Just like in the alphabet, F comes before G: FAITH, FAMILY, and FRIENDS, then golf.

Just Do It

If I claimed to love golf yet I never played, never practiced, did not watch it on television, did not subscribe to Golf Digest, did not tell golf stories, and had rust on my clubs, I dare say you would doubt my commitment.

Sometimes we claim to have a Spiritual faith and don't attend services, don't study our faith, don't talk about it, and almost seem embarrassed to admit a professing faith. Christ says the commandments are all found in six words: " Love God and love your neighbor."

The Gospel, according to Nike, I like: "Just Do It."

I've Got a Chance

September and October are the prime months for benefit golf tournaments. For many years, my golf buddies and I were a golfing force to be reckoned with by all comers. We all hit the ball a long way, and we could putt like crazy.

As we are all reaching the 70s, we still play, but winning opportunities are limited to putting green and drawings for door prizes. Many older golfers may want to leave these tournaments with the young guys., but I am with the Apostle Paul who said in Galatians 6:9, "so let us not grow weary in doing what is right and good, for we will reap at harvest time if we do not give up."

So, Paul, you're saying, "I've got a chance,"

Giving Advice

Giving golf tips to another golfer is tricky. A good rule of thumb is to avoid advice from anyone whose handicap is significantly more than yours and never give advice to someone with a single digit handicap. The most important rule of advice giving is never giving golf instruction to your spouse unless you are asked and know even when you are asked, there is great potential for discord.

The most important thing to remember when giving advice about golf or life is that there is a vast difference between putting your nose in other people's business and putting your heart in other people's problems.

What Did You Hit on 14?

My friend Holly, a true Southern gentleman and former golf pro, tells a wonderful story of one of his club members who Invariably searched for Holly after every round of golf and related to Holly a shot-by-shot description of his entire round. The club member was elderly and much loved, and Holly never felt he could cut the man off once the story had begun.

One day as the man finished hole #3, Holly interjected, "What did you hit off the tee on #14?"

Miraculously the storyteller skipped to 14 and finished the round from there. Until Holly left the club, he used his serendipitous discovery to shorten his listening time, but seemingly never offended the teller. Storytelling is a wonderful talent, but listening is the skill that changes people's lives. God help me listen to you and to others today.

Eternity Foursome

My oldest son developed a love for golf during the summer after his sophomore year at college. He worked in the golf pro shop during the day, and after work, we played many rounds of golf.

During one of our evening father-son "bonding" rounds as we called them, we started talking about who we wouldn't mind playing golf with for eternity. (All golfers assume there are golf courses in heaven.) David and I decided to call those people "eternity" people.

What a compliment to think that someone might put you on their eternity foursome. It made me stop and think. Am I the kind of person that others would want to spend eternity with? What are the characteristics of an eternity person?

That famous golfer St. Paul pointed them out in his letter to the golf club at Galatia: love, Joy, Peace, patience, kindness, goodness, faithfulness and self-control! Would anyone choose you for an eternity person? Would they choose me?

Best Scores

Have you ever added up your lowest score on each hole of your golf course? One Sunday morning, I was daydreaming during the sermon and started adding up my best scores. On my par 72 home course, my optimum score now stands at 47. A mere 25 under par. I shared this discovery with a friend of mine and made the statement that by adding up my low scores, I now felt it was theoretically possible for me to go out and shoot 25 under par. My friend patiently listened to my entire spiel and then said, "Have you added up your worst scores."

I don't know about you, but I am not adding up my worst scores. First of all, I have tried to erase them all from my memory bank. (I do remember making a 13 on one hole in the club championship, but that was too good of a story to forget.) I know in my heart I am capable of a lot of bad. Our time on earth is too short to spend focusing on the negatives of life. Who wants to remember bad shots and bad days?

Today's prayer is maybe today, I can add a best day to my life score.

It's Not the Arrow

Golfers are fickle about their clubs. We love them, but we always have a roaming eye for something better. I was with my friend Phil, and I was having trouble with my new three wood. I took his three wood out of his bag and hit it perfectly. I promptly claimed his club.

Phil didn't want to trade until he hit my club in the screws. Then the deal was done.

Unlike swapping golf clubs, making a life change can be and is usually stressful. It is the story of the universe. We adapt and change, or we don't survive.

My whispered prayer today is "Lord help me know when it is time to let go of the old and try the new and please don't let my 25-year-old putter go south on me because I may be too old to break in another one."

Friendships

In 1999, my dad and I played the old course at *St. Andrews*. In the pro shop I discovered a bottle of single malt scotch distilled In the town of St. Andrews. It came in a wooden box with the logo of the Old Course on the front. I brought the bottle home and my golf group all etched their names on the wooden box. Our commitment is to gather at the demise of each of us and take a sip of the scotch and remember.

We broke the seal and sipped when Mikey passed. We hope it will be a good while before the next taste. Pasted to the back of the box is a toast we raise at the end of our gatherings. One day it will be raised by only one. The Toast:

Here's to The friendships Created and
Nurtured by the mutual
love for the game of golf.
To the players and the game.

CPSIA information can be obtained
at www.ICGtesting.com
Printed in the USA
LVHW040917150920
665955LV00004B/8

9 781733 313001